Threatened Cultures

INUIT

Bryan and Cherry Alexander

RSVP
RAINTREE
STECK-VAUGHN
P U B L I S H E R S
The Steck-Vaughn Company
Austin, Texas

Titles in the Series

Australian Aborigines
Bedouin
Inuit
Rain Forest Amerindians

Series editors: Paul Mason and Pam Wells
Designer: Kudos Editorial and Design Services

All photographs in this book are
© Bryan and Cherry Alexander

Library of Congress Cataloging-in-Publication Data
Alexander, Bryan.
    Inuit / Bryan and Cherry Alexander.
      p. cm. — (Threatened cultures)
    Includes bibliographical references and index.
    Summary: Discusses the Inuit and their continuing
struggle to preserve their way of life and maintain their
cultural identity in the modern world.
    ISBN 0-8114-2301-8
    1. Eskimos—Juvenile literature. [1. Eskimos—Ethnic
identity. 2. Indians of North America—Ethnic identity.]
I. Alexander, Cherry. II. Title. III. Series.
E99.E7A488 1993
973'.04971—dc20   92-9894
                              CIP AC

Printed by Lego, Italy
Bound in the United States by Lake Book, Melrose Park, IL

1 2 3 4 5 6 7 8 9 0 LB 98 97 96 95 94 93

Contents

1 Introduction

Viewed from space the Arctic is clearly visible as an irregular patch of white sitting on the top of our planet. It looks white because it is covered by ice and snow. The Arctic is a place of extreme cold, where it seems unlikely that you would find animals, let alone people. But this frozen wilderness is home to the Inuit.

The Inuit have lived along the northern-most coasts of Siberia, Alaska, Canada, and Greenland for thousands of years. Over this time they have developed a way of life that allows them to survive in the extreme cold and to live off the Arctic's abundant wildlife. The traditional life-style of the Inuit as nomadic hunter-gatherers proved so successful that they were able to expand across the polar region.

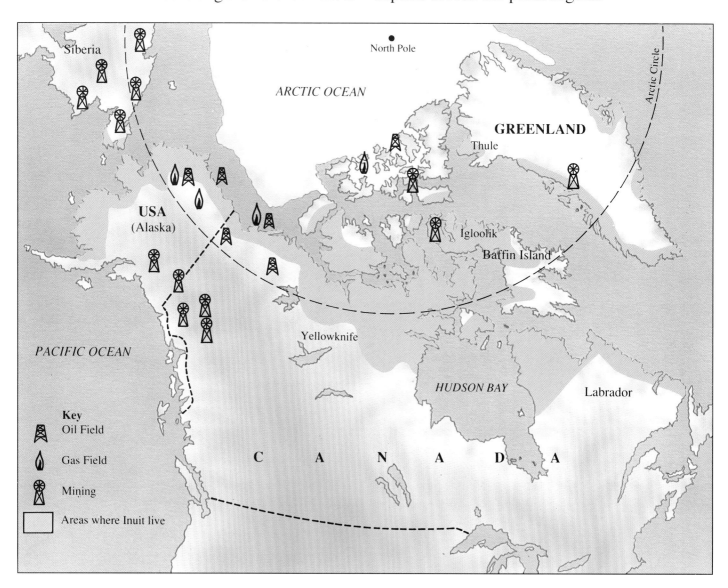

▲ The areas where the Inuit live, and the location of oil and gas fields, and mines.

Polar Night and Midnight Sun

Because the Earth is slightly tilted on its axis, the area above the Arctic Circle faces away from the sun during the winter months and tilts towards the sun during the summer. This is why during the summer there are periods of time when the sun never sets below the horizon, a phenomenon often referred to as the midnight sun. During the winter there is an equivalent number of days when the sun never appears above the horizon, a period which is known as the polar night. The further north you travel above the Arctic Circle the longer these periods of continuous sunlight and darkness become. The picture above shows the midnight sun.

The northernmost natural Inuit community in the world is Thule in northwest Greenland. There the sun stays above the horizon from the end of April until the end of August. Then in the autumn the sun sets in late October and is not seen again until the middle of the following February.

Aurora Borealis

The "northern lights" are one of the most spectacular sights of the winter months in the Arctic. These translucent moving curtains of light hang in the night sky. Constantly changing, they dance across the cold night skies in colors from white and green to red.

For a long time the cause of these spectacular displays of light remained a mystery. Some indigenous peoples of the Arctic believed they were the dancing spirits of their ancestors. Scientists discovered that the lights are caused by electrons from the sun colliding with molecules of gases in the Earth's upper atmosphere. The lights are so spectacular in the Arctic and Antarctic because more electrons are attracted to the magnetic poles of the Earth.

▲　The "northern lights" or aurora borealis appear like a curtain of light in the Arctic's winter sky.

There are around 100,000 Inuit in the world today. Hunting is still crucial to the survival of their culture, but many aspects of their lives have changed. The indigenous peoples of the Arctic are no longer the only ones who can survive the extreme cold. The Arctic is rich in natural resources, and Europeans and North Americans have developed the necessary technologies to exploit the Arctic lands and seas that the Inuit once had to themselves.

The challenges for today's Inuit are preserving their land and making their cultural identity strong enough to withstand the increasing pressures of the modern world.

▲ British Petroleum's main production island at Endicott, Prudhoe Bay, Alaska.

2 Inuit - The People

THE SPIRIT WORLD

In the past, the Inuit did not worship gods. Instead they believed that everything that moved possessed a spirit. This included the animals and birds they hunted. Unlike many other religions, theirs did not make a distinction between animals and people. As a result of this belief, they had great respect for nature. From their viewpoint it would be foolish not to respect the spirits of the animals they hunted. If they didn't observe certain acts of courtesy to the dead animal, these animals would not allow themselves to be hunted in the future, and bad luck would come to the hunter and his family.

▲ Walruses have always been prized by the Inuit. They provide tasty meat, and their ivory tusks can be used to make sled runners, harpoons, needles, carvings, and toys.

▲   The Inuit believe in living in harmony with nature. They do not overhunt animals, as the whalers did in the Arctic seas during the nineteenth century. They know that if they did there would soon be no animals left to hunt.

The Inuit believed that having a proper attitude was as important to the success of a hunt as the actual skill of the hunter. When beheading a dead animal to release its spirit, the hunter asks the spirit to return to the wild. Another common practice was to return some small part of a marine mammal to the sea, both for the benefit of the animal's spirit and to encourage rebirth. An animal that was respected would allow itself to be killed again when it occupied its next body.

The Inuit lived in a complicated world of spirits that had to be appeased, and so they practiced a variety of rituals designed to ensure the success of their lives. To communicate with the spirit world, the Inuit used the services of an *angakkuq* (shaman). By entering into a trance the *angakkuq* would be able to see if a hunt would be successful or whether a taboo had been broken.

An *angakkuq* was also consulted when a newborn baby was to be named. To the Inuit, a person's name is far more than just the label it is in our society. They used to believe that by naming a child after someone who had recently died they were inviting that person's spirit to enter the newborn baby. The spirit then influenced the life of that child. Because there were both good and evil spirits looking for bodies to enter, an *angakkuq* would be called upon to advise the parents which names of good spirits were available and which evil ones to avoid. Recently a popular and great hunter died in an accident. Five months after his death six babies have been given his name, *Ituko*, and his spirit lives on in the community.

▼   An Inuit girl well-wrapped in caribou furs to protect her from the severe winter cold.

▲ Seal skins drying on a hunter's meat rack in Greenland. When they are ready they can be used for clothing.

▼ Most Inuit's main source of food is animals they have hunted. This hunter is chopping polar bear meat.

FOOD

Because the Arctic region remains frozen for most of the year, it is not possible to grow vegetables or grains like wheat there. The traditional Inuit diet consists almost exclusively of meat, fat, and fish. In the past their whole life revolved around the constant search for food. Out of necessity the Inuit have always had to use what little the Arctic had to offer. Their main food is seal, but they also eat caribou, walrus, polar bear, musk-oxen, whales, arctic hare, fish, and birds. Many Inuit now also eat convenience foods, which they buy from shops in the settlements where they they live.

▲   These Inuit are shopping in a store in Igloolik, Canada. Most Inuit now supplement their traditional meat diet with food from stores.

After a kill, the meat and fat of an animal is either eaten raw or boiled. If the Inuit kill more animals than they can eat, they store some of the meat to feed themselves when there is not as much game around. During the winter months meat never spoils because it is always so cold. In the summer months the Inuit preserve meat either by using the wind to dry it or by storing it under rocks. The Inuit waste very little of any animal they kill. Fat, meat and internal organs are all eaten.

So, if they do not eat fruit and vegetables, where do the Inuit get their vitamins from? Surprisingly, a diet of meat and fat provides everything a human needs to have a healthy life. In fact, recent medical surveys show that the Inuit who still eat mainly meat are healthier in many ways than people who eat a mixture of meat and vegetables. Heart disease, diabetes, and cancer are all rare among the Inuit. Just because they do not have fruit and vegetables does not mean the Inuit are lacking in vitamins. Seal liver and whale skin are rich in vitamins and contain the same proportion of Vitamin C as is found in grapefruit.

Over the past 25 years the Inuit diet has undergone considerable change. Shops in northern communities now stock an increasing amount of convenience food, which has resulted in many Inuit eating foods that are rich in carbohydrates and sugar. Some Inuit have begun to develop tooth decay and a whole range of diet-related diseases that were unknown before. A diet that many of us would consider to be normal has introduced the Inuit to new diseases and worse health.

It was the use of furs and the invention of the needle that allowed the Inuit's ancestors to make clothing that shielded them from the lethal cold. Over the past few hundred years the style of the Inuit's winter fur clothing has remained nearly unchanged. Although there are regional variations, the basic principle of Inuit clothing is the same throughout the Arctic. A double layer of skin clothes is worn, with the fur of the inside layer facing in and the fur of the outside layer facing out. In the Canadian North the fur clothing is mainly from caribou. In Greenland there are more variations. The skins of seal, polar bear, caribou, and arctic fox are all used to make winter clothes.

In shops throughout the Arctic today, there is a variety of modern clothing available to the Inuit. Young Inuit like fashionable clothes. In their villages they wear jeans, brightly colored sportswear and sneakers. However, when it comes to going out hunting in the middle of winter, many Inuit still rely on traditional fur clothing. No modern substitute has proved as warm and durable.

HOUSING

One of the myths about the Inuit is that they all live in snow houses called igloos. For most Inuit these snow houses were never more than temporary shelters that they built on hunting trips during the winter months. In fact the word for a snow house in their language is *illuviga*. Igloo (*illu*) just means a house of any kind. Their traditional winter homes were built half underground and made using rocks and clumps of earth. Whale bones were often used as rafters and the walls lined with skins for insulation. When the Inuit moved to summer camps, they lived in tents made from seal or caribou skins.

Although housing in the Arctic varies from country to country, most Inuit now live in one-story prefabricated wood houses. They are heated by oil-burning stoves and have a

▼ An Inuit hunter building a snow house (*illuviga*) to spend the night in. Hunters use these as temporary shelters.

▲ Most Inuit now live in settlements. This is Iqualit on Baffin Island. The homes are flown in ready-made from the south.

combined kitchen and living area, and one or two separate bedrooms. In the Canadian North water is brought to the houses once or twice a week by a community truck. Another truck removes sewage in plastic bags known locally as honey bags. Flush toilets are still unusual in many of the Arctic's Inuit communities.

THE SEASONAL CYCLE

The seasonal changes in a land that is always covered by snow and ice are hard for an outsider to spot. To the Inuit the change from the bitter cold of – 49 °F in early February and the +14 °F of May is as different as summer and winter are to us, even though the ice and snow are there all the time.

Each Inuit community has evolved its own seasonal cycle. Hunters must react to seasonal changes and the movements of the animals they depend on for most of their food. Each spring

the herds of walruses move north, following the edge of the shrinking pack ice. At this time herds of caribou migrate to their summer pastures, where they will have their young.

Summer is the time of camps, when whole

The Inuit Languages

You might be surprised to discover that you already know one or two words of the Inuit language. Words like *anorak*, *kayak*, and *igloo* have found their way into English. The Inuit speak two main languages, and there are many regional dialects of these spoken across the Arctic. The Inuit of Siberia and southwest Alaska speak *yupik*, while in the rest of Alaska, Canada, and Greenland they speak *inuktitut*. They call themselves Inuit, which is usually translated as real people or human beings. Inuk is the singular form. They prefer this name to Eskimo, which comes from an Algonquin word meaning "He eats [meat] raw."

An Inuk from north Greenland catches little auks with a long-handled net. During the summer there is an abundance of food.

Inuit families move out of their villages to make the most of the great variety of food this season has to offer. There are the eggs and meat from the millions of seabirds that arrive to feed in the plankton-rich waters of the Arctic. Arctic char, a type of trout, are caught as they enter the rivers and lakes to spawn. Whales are hunted in the fjords, which are only free of ice in the summer.

It is a time to put food aside for the winter ahead.

In the autumn the days shorten and the seas begin to freeze. The Inuit overhaul their dogsleds and snowmobiles so they are ready for when the ice is thick enough for them to venture out on to it to hunt seals at their breathing holes. Even when the sun has set for the winter, the Inuit continue to hunt during the polar night.

An Inuit hunter on Baffin Island during April prepares to skin and butcher a caribou he has just shot. ▶

In the spring the ice begins to rot and hunting becomes dangerous. Many Inuit fish through holes in the ice for arctic char. They also fish at other times of the year.

Surprisingly, after the sun's return the coldest time of the year begins. As more of the sea freezes, the hunter's territory increases. Inuit hunters make long journeys in search of polar bear, seal, and walrus. Gradually the days lengthen, and, as the sun gets higher in the sky, it becomes warmer. Hunters stalk the seals that drag themselves up on to the ice to bask in the spring sunshine. Hunting can be difficult in July because the sea ice becomes too soft to travel on but still prevents them from using boats or kayaks. Some hunters resort to fishing through holes in the fast-melting ice, hoping each day that a storm will blow it away.

16

Whether they live in a town or a village, the Inuit think that "land food" is preferable to "shop food." "To buy cans from the store you need money," one Inuit woman told me. Inuit living in the larger settlements face restrictions on what they can hunt. Many of the animals that lived close to these towns have either been killed already or have moved away from such a dangerous area. So the hunters may have to travel for many hours to find seals or caribou. But they still continue to hunt, though often on a part-time basis. In Igloolik, a town in the Canadian Arctic, a returning hunter often announces over the local radio that he has meat to share with his friends and family.

Inuit Art

The picture above shows Mabel Nigayath, from Holman Island, working on a print of one of her drawings. Over the past 40 years the Inuit have become famous for their art. They carve figures usually in soapstone, but they also use bone and ivory. Some communities produce pictures, too. Much Inuit art depicts the animals they depend on and scenes of traditional life. Their art is based on their knowledge of nature, gained after many years of living off the land. Most communities in northern Canada have cooperatives that buy the work from the artist and send it to southern galleries. Holman Island and Cape Dorset have become particularly famous for their art. Cape Dorset's 900 Inuit residents produce more than $4,000,000 worth of sculptures and prints each year.

3 Qallunaaq - White People

THE EXPLORERS

Imagine being one of a small group of people who had become so isolated that they believed they were the only people on earth. Then one day two enormous ships—something you had never seen before—arrived, full of people who looked and dressed differently from you and spoke a language you could not understand. Would you be afraid?

Now perhaps you can understand how the Inuit of North Greenland must have felt when the Scottish explorer John Ross arrived at Cape York in the summer of 1818. He was among the first to search for the Northwest Passage, a shortcut to the East.

The American explorers Robert Peary and Matthew Henson, and four Inuit reached the

◀ The first white explorers were helped in their travels by Inuit. The explorers used Inuit sleds and dogs very like the one this man is on.

North Pole in April 1909. Peary, who claimed that he was the first to reach the pole, used the Inuit dogs and sleds as transportation. It must have been hard for the Inuit to understand why explorers like Peary wanted to go through so much hardship just to reach some remote geographical point where the ice was too thick to hunt seals. Even so, the Inuit welcomed the arrival of these people in their great ships. This gave them the opportunity to trade and to be paid for their help with needles, knives, and—most prized of all—wood. (Trees do not grow in the Arctic.)

◀ The grave of Alex Elder. He was a crew member on Edward Parry's second voyage in search of the Northwest Passage, which was made from 1821 - 23.

Minik

In 1897 the American explorer Robert Peary took four Inuit from north Greenland to New York City. Among them was a seven-year-old boy called Minik and his father Qisuk. Within five months Qisuk died, leaving Minik as an orphan in a foreign land. Peary offered to take Minik back to Greenland, but Minik chose to remain in this country. He was later adopted by an American. Minik grew up here and years later went home as part of another expedition.

THE WHALERS

In the early nineteenth century, oil that was needed for heat, light, and lubrication didn't come from underground wells. It came from whales. Whales also provided baleen (whalebone) which was used in the manufacture of a whole range of goods, from women's corsets to fishing rods. Whalebone was the plastic of the nineteenth century.

Once the whalers discovered that during the summer months the Arctic's coastal waters were full of whales, more and more ships and men headed up to the north each year. The Inuit nicknamed them *Upernaallit*, which means those who arrive in spring. The whalers began to change the Inuit culture. They traded with the Inuit, and their valuable new goods, such as rifles, knives, and tools became indispensable. They took the Inuit out of the Stone Age forever.

Over 500 whaling ships were wrecked in the Arctic's treacherous ice and sea. Those that were washed ashore provided the Inuit with valuable supplies of metal and wood. Some whaling companies used the Inuit in their crews, but mainly the Inuit men hunted for fresh meat for the sailors. The Inuit women sewed fur clothes and sleeping bags for the sailors.

Seal Hunting

In the U.S. many people want to protect seals because they seem cuddly and friendly, rather than because they are endangered. The Inuit mainly hunt adult seals in a humane way using rifles. Does it make sense to deny the Inuit the opportunity to market their sealskins when they will kill seals anyway for food? Do we have the right to tell a people with a culture much older than ours, who have always looked after their environment, how to run their lives? There are over ten million seals in the Arctic seas. The main threat to their existence comes from pollution, not Inuit hunters.

◄ An old print of British whalers off the coast of Greenland. The whalers hunted the whales close to extinction, then they left.

The Inuit adopted the whalers' music and learned to play the concertina and accordion. Rock music and country and western are popular with young Inuit these days. Much of the Inuit music and dancing that is considered traditional is based on Scottish reels and was learned many years ago from the whalers who visited the Arctic.

During the 100 years that European and American whalers operated in the Arctic they slaughtered nearly all the bowhead whales. When these became scarce, they moved on to smaller whales and walruses. When they had killed almost all the wildlife that the Inuit depended on, the whalers departed, leaving the Inuit to face starvation.

THE FUR TRADERS

The next group to venture into the Arctic were the fur traders. They, like the whalers before them, were motivated by greed. Companies like the famous Hudson's Bay Company were quick to exploit the large profits that could be made from northern furs, particularly of foxes, in Europe and the East.

The Inuit became increasingly dependent on white people's goods. By the early 1900s they were using rifles, knives, saws, hatchets, telescopes, drills, files, sewing needles, and thread, in addition to cooking pots and other utensils. They had also acquired a taste for tobacco, coffee, tea, and flour. All these things they obtained by trading furs. The fur trade had

▲ Having initially encouraged the Inuit to trap animals for furs, many Westerners now claim that the fur trade is wrong. The Inuit kill animals for food. Do you think they should be able to sell the furs?

a great effect on the Inuit; it changed their seasonal cycle. Each autumn when the trapping season began, their main activity was to trap foxes for fur instead of hunting for meat. They no longer hunted only what they needed to live; the Inuit had become trappers.

MISSIONARIES

After the fur traders came the missionaries. Several different Christian groups, such as Catholic, Anglican, Lutheran, and Protestants, began to build missions and churches all over the North. These different groups competed for Inuit converts. They introduced the idea that you could dislike someone because of her or his religion and devalued the old ways by saying that Christianity was better. Like the whalers before them, they altered the traditional way of life of the Inuit. By introducing Christian morals and values the missionaries undermined many traditional beliefs. Customs like shamanism and the belief in the spirit world almost disappeared. To what extent the Inuit really adopted Christianity is difficult to say. In some Inuit communities even today, beliefs about the spirit world linger on.

◀ ▲ The picture above is of the Anglican church in Igloolik, and the one on the left is of the Catholic church. By introducing Christian values the missionaries undermined and devalued traditional beliefs.

SETTLEMENT

After World War II came the Cold War and the fear of a Soviet attack from across the Arctic Ocean. This resulted in the rapid building of military DEW (distant early warning) stations in a line across the top of North America and Greenland. Many Inuit left their traditional hunting grounds to work as laborers at the Dewline sites. But, when the work was completed and they were no longer needed, some found it difficult to return to the life of a hunter. Instead they stayed near the sites or moved to the growing settlements.

Up until the 1950s the Canadian government had taken little interest in its northern lands and people. But reports of disease and starvation in Inuit communities changed this, and the

▲ Inuit children playing ice hockey in the street. Many Inuit moved to settlements in the 1950s because their children had to go to school in the towns.

government began a relocation program. The Inuit were lured and pressured to leave their camps, which were scattered across the North and move to makeshift settlements.

One reason why they settled in towns was that their children were taken away from the camps to go to school in the towns, so the families moved into town to be close to them. This marked the end of the traditional nomadic life-style for almost all Inuit. From this time on, most lived in communities where they were given free housing, health care, and an education

◀ The Trans-Alaska Pipeline, which carries the equivalent of two million barrels of oil a day. The oil and mining companies are the latest group to occupy land that the Inuit have used for many generations.

that was designed to prepare the Inuit to work for a living in the same way that people in the West do.

The jobs the Inuit were led to believe they would find in the settlements were few and far between. Those that there were, with the government, often proved temporary. Most Inuit ended up living on welfare payments and government support programs. They had given up their self-sufficient life of hunting, trapping, and fishing for one of increasing dependence on modern society.

When oil and gas were first discovered in northern Alaska in 1968, the Inuit people realized that there was a very real risk that the lands they depended on would be destroyed by an industry whose only aim was to remove the oil and ship it south for profit. If they were to maintain any control over the use of their lands, they would need the government in the south to recognize their rights. The threat posed by mining and drilling was certainly instrumental in starting the land claim negotiations. Throughout the North Inuit groups asked that oil not be moved either by pipeline or icebreaking tanker. They wanted to know what effect the oil business and its pollution would have on the lives of caribou and seals on which the Inuit depended.

4 Igloolik - Place of Houses

Most of Canada's Inuit live in the province known as the Northwest Territories. This vast and seemingly empty land is the size of a small continent and consists of thousands of headlands and islands, some larger than European countries. It is in the northeast of this region on a small island in Foxe Basin that the community of Igloolik, which means place of houses, lies. The Igloolik district has been occupied by the Inuit for at least 4,000 years.

Igloolik was first visited by Europeans in 1822 when the British explorer Edward Parry arrived with two ships, the *Fury* and *Hecla*. But it was not until more than a hundred years later in 1939, when a Hudson's Bay Company trading post was established there, that Igloolik began

▲ The Inuit village of Igloolik in the Canadian Arctic.

▲ Shoppers outside the Hudson's Bay Company store in Igloolik.

to undergo great changes. Almost overnight it became the most important settlement in Foxe Basin.

The opening of a military DEW (distant early warning) station 60 miles south at Hall Beach in 1956 brought improved transport and communications with other places. Soon Igloolik was to become a government administration center with a school, nursing station, and Royal Canadian Mounted Police unit. Lured by the promise of homes where heat and light came with the flick of a switch, and by medical care and schooling for their children, the Inuit abandoned their nomadic camp life for the settlement of Igloolik. Now only a handful of families still spend the whole year out on the

land, while the settlement has grown into a community of 1,000. Like many other northern Inuit communities it consists mainly of rows of single story prefabricated houses. These are brought to the Arctic by ship each summer, along with other supplies.

In Igloolik today you find a mixture of traditional Inuit culture with the influences of Western culture. Now snowmobiles and three-wheelers, the modern transport of the Arctic, speed along the same tracks as dogsleds. In the porches of the Inuit homes fashionable, brightly-colored skiwear can be found hanging alongside traditional caribou-skin clothing.

Even though only 1,000 people live in Igloolik, there are facilities that you would only expect to

◀ Life for the Inuit of Igloolik is a mixture of traditional and modern. People still hunt, but they are as likely to hunt from snowmobiles as from dogsleds.

find in a much larger town. These include an ice hockey and curling rink, community hall, swimming pool, library, and playground. Igloolik has its own small radio station, which broadcasts news, music, and messages twice a day. Televisions and videos are to be found in almost every home and the local shops stock the same range of video films that can be found the world over.

Three hundred children attend classes at Igloolik's modern and well-equipped *Attagutaluk* school. The school has a large gym and a computer studies room with twenty-two computers that would be the envy of any similar-sized community in the United States.

Missionaries have been at Igloolik for over fifty years, bringing with them different kinds of Christianity. Each religion has its own group

Igloolik has a modern school. These children are using a computer that is programmed in *inuktitut.* ▶

Inuit hunters eating raw arctic char. Despite the increasing availability of modern convenience food, many Inuit still rely for food on caribou, seal, walrus, fish, and polar bear that they have caught themselves.

of followers. The Catholics live on the north side of the village near their church, while the Anglicans live on the south side near theirs. This division splits the community in two. Not long ago relations between these two religious groups were not good. Leah Otak, an Inuit woman who comes from a devout Anglican family, told me, "When I was in my teens, if I so much as looked at a Catholic boy, I would get into big trouble at home."

Although it is an isolated community 298 miles above the Arctic Circle, Igloolik has two remarkably well-stocked shops. Fresh fruit and vegetables are flown in on the twice-weekly flights that link Igloolik with the rest of Canada. The shelves of the stores are stacked with TV dinners, hamburgers, cookies, potato chips, sodas and a wide variety of other junk foods. Prices are high. Most foods in Igloolik cost between 30 and 70 percent more than in southern Canada. Most of the Inuit still rely on the traditional staple "land foods" such as caribou, seal, walrus, and arctic char.

Although there are only about forty full-time hunters among the Inuit of Igloolik these days, practically everyone hunts on a part-time basis. On a fine spring Friday afternoon you will see a procession of snowmobiles and dogsleds leaving town. They are carrying people across the sea ice for a weekend's seal hunting, in the same way as people leave any southern city for a weekend in the country. The Inuit will take coffee, sugar, and hardtack with them, but seldom carry meat, as it would mean a lack of confidence in their ability to hunt.

The sea around Igloolik is only free of ice for eight to ten weeks of the year. The Inuit who live there make the most of this brief Arctic summer. In early August, after the ice breaks in Foxe Basin, Igloolik almost empties as families leave to go out on the land, to hunt and fish from camping sites that they return to year after year.

The people of Igloolik, as in all Canadian Arctic communities, have become dependent on the government. It provides the houses in which people live, education, medical services, law enforcement, telephones, and money — all essential for life in the Arctic today.

After eight or more years of schooling many

▼   An Inuit hunter prepares to camp out for the night on the ice sea.

Outpost Camps

Even though it is very difficult to earn a living from hunting these days, some Inuit families still choose to turn their backs on the amenities and bright lights of Igloolik. They spend the whole year living off the land at isolated camps. Under the Canadian government's Outpost Camp program those families who want to return to the traditional life on the land can claim both financial and material help.

young people emerge to find that the one thing that the government doesn't provide is enough jobs. Unemployment in Igloolik is between 70 and 80 percent. Most of the jobs that do exist are low-paying government jobs for the community, such as driving snowplows or honey wagons, or working as classroom assistants. Most young Inuit are unwilling and probably unable to live entirely by hunting, although they still hunt part-time for extra food. They end up without the jobs they have been educated for and unwilling to live in the way their grandparents did—off the land. The only way for them to survive is on welfare payments from the government.

Pollution from industrialized southern cities has spread to the farthest corners of the Arctic. In the same way, the problems of southern

With his harpoon ready, an Inuit hunter waits above a breathing hole. Very few Inuit now live entirely by hunting, but nearly all hunt part-time. ▶

▲ Snowmobiles parked outside an Inuit home.

societies have spread even to remote settlements like Igloolik. Alcoholism has been a problem in communities throughout the North for a long time, but for the Inuit it has become much more of a problem over the last twenty years.

In an attempt to combat the problem of alcoholism, some communities declared that no alcohol would be allowed at all. In others, like Igloolik, alcohol cannot be sold, and you can only buy it from outside the village. More recently, drugs and solvent abuse have become problems among the Inuit youth. The schools are trying to help solve the problem by teaching their students about the dangers of drugs and solvent abuse.

Despite its problems Igloolik has the reputation of being a very united and independent-minded community. It is seen by many as a stronghold of Inuit culture. Over the past decade many of the leaders of campaigns for Inuit rights have come from Igloolik.

Alcohol and the Fur Trade

In the early days of the fur trade Inuit hunters were offered alcohol when they traded furs. The people who gave them the alcohol hoped that the Inuit would become dependent on it. Then they would have to trap more animals for skins to get more alcohol.

5 The Hunters

After harpooning a whale an Inuit hunter from north Greenland told me, "As I got close to the whale, my heart was beating so loudly I thought the whale would hear it and dive." There is a great feeling of tension and excitement during a hunt. It is the same feeling that a young boy or girl fishing beside a river has when a fish tugs at the line. It is an innate part of all of us—a legacy of our hunting ancestry.

Hunting cultures are dying out in other parts of the world. It might be exciting, but do the Inuit really need to hunt in the 1990s? The Inuit live in an area of the world where there is no agriculture and little industry. They have few employment possibilities. Hunting is vital to the Inuit, because it is central to their culture and also provides them with food and clothing.

Today Inuit hunters follow the seasonal movements of their main prey — caribou, seal, polar bear, walrus, and whales. The life of a hunter in today's Arctic is still hard and often dangerous, and a successful hunter frequently takes risks. Every year there are cases of hunters being killed when they fall through thin ice or are swept out to sea on an ice floe. Modern technology has in some ways made hunting easier. In most parts of the Arctic the snowmobile (a motorized scooter that can pull a sled) has

▲ "As I got close to the whale, my heart was beating so loudly I thought the whale would hear it and dive."

◀ An Inuit hunter uses his dogs to help haul the heavy carcass of a walrus he has killed on to the ice.

replaced the dog team, and hunters use rifles, binoculars, motor boats, canvas tents, camping stoves, and fishing nets. The Inuit are expert at taking things from Western society and incorporating them into their own culture. They use nylon sled runners, since nylon offers little friction on snow and ice; some use cotton wool instead of grass as insulation in their boots. Dental floss is used to sew leather because it has similar properties to the traditional thread they made from the muscle sinew of a whale.

With the introduction of high-powered rifles equipped with telescopic sights, the Inuit could have wiped out the animals they hunt. But they are aware of the need to conserve animal populations for future generations of hunters. They never want to have to apologize to their grandchildren for the fact that there are no animals left to hunt. In the past the size of a hunting community was no larger than the

In the spring, seals haul themselves on to the ice. Inuit hunters in Greenland stalk these seals using fabric screens to hide themselves. ▶

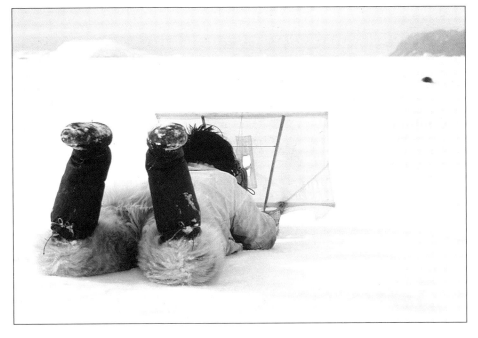

An Inuit measures the tusks of a dead walrus. By supplying biologists with information about the animals they hunt, the Inuit are helping scientists to find out more about these creatures.

number of people that could live on the animals in the area. To kill too many animals was short sighted. The Inuit would soon have nothing to eat and have to find somewhere else to live.

Before Christianity destroyed many of their old beliefs in the spirit world, the Inuit had taboos that prevented over-hunting. There was a taboo against killing more than five foxes in one day. The Greenland Inuit believed that if too many seals were killed at the same place, a group of seals in human form would come in a boat of ice to take revenge. It was the fear of offending the spirits of the animals they hunted that made the Inuit observe these taboos.

Various hunting restrictions have now replaced taboos, and these vary from region to region. In the Thule district of northwest Greenland hunting from snowmobiles is banned, so the dogsled is still the only form of winter transport for hunting. In some fjords hunting from motorboats is banned, and the Inuit hunt whales from a kayak using a hand harpoon. A date is set each year when the Inuit are allowed to collect down and eggs from Eider duck colonies. This is done early enough in the season to allow the ducks to lay a second nest of eggs. The local hunter's council meets every two or three months to enforce the hunting regulations, which are designed to conserve the wildlife of the area and preserve the Inuit culture.

The lives of Inuit hunters were never easy, but in recent years they have been faced with a new set of problems. As hunting has become more mechanized, the cost of equipment like rifles, snowmobiles, outboard motors, and boats has increased. At the same time the price of sealskins has gone down dramatically. An Inuit hunter now finds it very difficult indeed to support a family and pay for expensive new hunting equipment.

The fall in the price of sealskins was the direct result of the public outcry over the annual cull of baby harp seals off the east coast of Canada. A campaign mounted by Greenpeace and other

▲ Modern weapons mean that the Inuit could easily wipe out the animals they hunt. In some places communities have decided that hunting should be done in the traditional way. Near Thule, Greenland, hunting from motorboats is banned.

▲ Hunting walrus during the summer in north Greenland

conservation groups was illustrated with gruesome photographs of baby seals being clubbed to death on the ice. There was such a public outcry that the U.S. government banned all sea mammal products from its markets. The European Economic Community (EEC) took similar action, banning the import of all seal products. Inevitably the market for sealskins collapsed. On average a sealskin that would have brought around $50 at a fur auction during the 1970s plummeted to $2.50 in 1982.

The collapse of the sealskin market meant that hunting communities across the Arctic faced economic disaster. Welfare officers throughout the North believe that the result of the Save the Seals campaign was that many more Inuit and other Native American hunters were forced to live off government benefit payments.

The Inuit had nothing to do with the harp seal cull or clubbing baby seals to death. They mainly hunt ringed seals. This is the most common seal in the Arctic with a population of between six and seven million. Not surprisingly, many Inuit felt angry that once again they were being told how to run their lives by Western governments that had little knowledge of Inuit life and not much to be proud of when it came to their own environmental protection history.

It wasn't the Inuit, they pointed out, who hunted whales to the edge of extinction. Nor are they responsible for the pollution that has spread into the remotest areas of the North. The Arctic sits at the center of a deadly whirlpool of poisons discarded by the rest of the world. The level of PCB's (a toxic chemical) found in polar bears quadrupled between 1969 and 1984. If current PCB inputs continue, the polar bears will exceed the limit classifying them as toxic waste by around the year 2005. The North has industrial effluent but no industry; PCB's but no refrigerators; DDT but no crop pests.

▼   If the pollution of the Arctic's seas continues to get worse, within twenty years the meat of seals, whales, and polar bears will be unfit for people to eat.   ▶

Nunavut - Our Land

▲ For many generations the Inuit were the only people in the Arctic. Now they are fighting to defend their land and their way of life.

In recent years increasing threats to the Inuit culture have come from a variety of outside sources. Animal rights groups opposed to the fur trade and seal hunting have undermined the Inuit hunting economy. Oil and gas development in the Arctic pose a serious threat to the environment their culture depends on. With improved communications and television programs from southern Canada and the U.S. coming into most Inuit homes, there is a risk of young Inuit losing their cultural identity and their language.

Although some classes in school are now taught in the local language, when schools were first introduced all lessons were in English, and the children did not learn in their own language. Most children now attend schools in their home towns and have some lessons in *inuktitut* or *yupik*, so the opportunities to continue using *inuktitut* are better, and it is now the main language for 80 percent of Inuit households.

There is a great lack of self-esteem among many Inuit today, especially the young people. Unemployment and enforced dependence on government aid does little to remove the feelings of inferiority and inequality that many Inuit have. Even when the Inuit are employed, most work in dull, low-paying jobs. White people in the North are never unemployed. They are the administrators and planners, the bosses and supervisors. White people not only have better jobs than the Inuit, they are also better paid, better housed, and better dressed. Yet it is the white people that are the intruders.

The rush to exploit the Arctic's oil, gas, and other mineral resources has led to an increasing number of industrial projects being set up in the North. With these came the promise of jobs for the Inuit, but the jobs often did not materialize. On most projects the Inuit made up under 5 percent of the work force. The opportunities to earn money that have come from these industrial schemes have proved short-term, with the Inuit poorly paid in comparison to other workers.

▲ For most communities in north Greenland, helicopters are the only link with other places during the winter.

◄ ▲ British Petroleum's facilities near Prudhoe Bay, Alaska. The main claims to Inuit lands now come from mineral exploration — mining, and petroleum and gas exploration all contribute to the pollution of the Arctic. There is a map on page four that shows where the main sites for this activity are.

▲ Siorapaluk, Greenland. Inuit political organizations negotiated Home Rule for Greenland in 1979.

When the projects ended, there was no more work. The economic and social effects on local communities were often disastrous. They destroyed the tradition of sharing and introduced Western ideas about owning things for their own sake, rather than because they were needed.

The Inuit have had to learn to adapt quickly. "In the last thirty years," a Canadian Inuk said, "we have gone from the Stone Age to the Middle Ages to the Space Age." One of the things that the Inuit learned quickly from white people is politics. Through their political leaders the Inuit have tried to put across their views and gain some control over their own future and lands. The Inuit political organizations have proved to be very persuasive. During the 1970s the Greenlanders expressed their dissatisfaction to the Danish government at being governed from abroad. By 1979 they had negotiated Home Rule. Although Greenland was to remain part of Denmark it would have the power to elect its own officials and run its own domestic affairs. In February 1985 it did just this and left the EEC.

Also during the 1970s the Inuit began negotiating with the governments of the U.S. and Canada for recognition that the land that they occupied and hunted over was theirs. They sought assurances that they and their land would be protected. The first of these land claims was made law in 1971 when the Alaska Native Claims Settlement awarded 44 million acres of land and over $900 million to the Aleuts, Inuit, and other Native Americans of Alaska.

Cooperatives

In 1959 the Inuit living in George River in northern Quebec borrowed money from the government to buy fishing boats, freezers, and other equipment they needed to start a commercial fishery. Other Inuit cooperatives followed. They used traditional skills, like making sealskin clothing or Inuit art, but most importantly they drew members of the community together. The cooperatives encourage people to rely on each other and share, in the way they did before the intrusion of Western values.

In recent years Inuit political leaders have been very successful in safeguarding Inuit rights, particularly regarding land claims. In Canada the Inuit may only be a small minority but they occupy one-third of the country. For the 17,000 Inuit living in the eastern and central Arctic, government acknowledgement of their rights has been achieved with a land claim known as *Nunavut*, which means "our land."

The original *Nunavut* claim was presented to the Canadian Government back in 1976. One of the earlier Inuit negotiators, James Arvaluk, dismissed the term "land claim." "The Inuit," he

▲ The Canadian Arctic. A huge area of land there is the subject of the *Nunavut* negotiations, in which the Inuit are claiming rights to the land they have occupied for generations.

▲ When *Nunavut* is agreed upon, Inuit will have control of the land on which they depend to keep their way of life alive.

said, "are claiming nothing. Rather we are offering to share our land with the rest of the Canadian population in return for recognition of rights and a say in the way the land is used and developed."

After fourteen years of negotiations, an Agreement in Principle was signed at a ceremony in Igloolik on April 30, 1990. The *Nunavut* claim is the largest land claim in Canadian history. Under its terms the Inuit receive title to 135,135 square miles of land, an area a little larger than Norway, with 14,000 square miles of underground mineral rights. They will also receive $580 million in compensation, which will be paid over fourteen years, and a share of any resource royalty payments received by the government. The Inuit will be actively involved in both wildlife management and local government.

Inuit Media

In Alaska, Canada, and Greenland the Inuit have their own newspapers, radio, and television programs. The Canadian government formed the Inuit Broadcasting Corporation (IBC) in 1981. It produces programs about the Inuit in their own language. These range from news and current affairs to documentaries on various aspects of Inuit life. Broadcasting television and radio programs to the Inuit in *inuktitut* will help preserve their culture and language.

▲ An Inuit artist at Holman Island in Canada's Northwest Territories hangs up a print to dry. Cooperatives have been started using money from land claims.

The *Nunavut* agreement was voted upon in May of 1992. This agreement has already done much to boost Inuit morale. Paul Irngaut, a young Inuk from Igloolik, said, "People are very optimistic here about *Nunavut*. It's exciting to think that we will have some control over our environment and wildlife."

It would be foolish to think that the *Nunavut* claim will be the answer to all the Inuit's problems. But as well as restoring their self-esteem, land claims like *Nunavut* will give

Financial Investment

Operating on a larger scale than the cooperatives is the *Inuvialuit* Development Corporation. It was founded in 1984 with some of the funds from the Alaskan *Inuvialuit* land claim agreement. For the first few years the Corporation did not make much money because the *Inuvialuit* did not have any experience in running a business. Now it is a well run business that makes money for all the members of the group.

them some economic independence. Some of the funds received from the claim will be used to start new local businesses that in turn will create jobs. Already Inuit cooperatives, set up to market local produce like fish, caribou meat, handicrafts, and art, have been set up right across the North and have proved successful in balancing the Inuit's traditional skills with modern economics. These Inuit cooperatives are the largest employer of indigenous labor in the Arctic.

The future of the Inuit would seem to lie in a mixed economy where people obtain their income from full- or part-time jobs, government welfare, and hunting, trapping, and fishing. The Inuit culture has always been flexible. Now they must earn cash because hunting alone cannot provide all the things they need. But they also recognize that without traditional hunting activities their culture cannot survive.

If the situation in the Arctic continues to develop in the same way as it has, it seems likely that within the next 20 years hunting of sea mammals and fishing by the Inuit will stop. This is unlikely to be the result of campaigns by animal rights organizations. It will be because by then the Arctic's seas will be so polluted that the meat from seals, whales, and polar bears will be unfit for people to eat.

The Inuit have a long struggle ahead of them if they are to preserve their unique culture and Arctic environment.

▼   The political battles the Inuit are now fighting will determine whether these children have a choice about how they want to live.

Glossary of English Words

Anglican Church   The Anglican Church of Canada developed from the Church of England.

Arctic char   A fish found in northern waters. It is similar to trout.

Baleen   The whalebone that grows in rows inside the mouths of large whales.

Caribou   North American reindeer.

Concertina   A portable musical instrument, somewhat like an accordian, that is popular with sailors.

Crustacean   An animal that usually lives in water and has a hard shell, such as a crab.

Cull   To kill animals of a particular species because there are too many of them.

DDT   A toxic chemical used to kill insects that eat farmers' crops.

Devout   Very religious.

EEC   European Economic Community. The nations of Western Europe joined together to create a single economic group.

Eider duck   A type of large duck found in northern waters. Its soft breast feathers, known as down, are used for stuffing quilts.

Ice floe   A sheet of floating ice.

Igloo   A dome-shaped shelter made from bricks of snow.

Indigenous   The first people to live in an area.

Kayak   A sealskin-covered canoe that is paddled sitting down, using a two-bladed oar.

Krill   Tiny crustaceans eaten by whales.

Leister   A fish spear.

Lutheran   A member of the Lutheran Church.

Migrate   To move yourself and your belongings from one place to another.

Musk-oxen   Long-haired, cattle-like animals with large curving horns.

Nomad   A person who lives in more than one place and travels from one to another at fixed times of the year.

Northwest passage   A passage for ships along the northern coast of North America. It was formerly thought of as a possible short-cut from Europe to the Far East.

PCB's   Polychlorinated biphenyls. Toxic chemicals used in lubricants and paints that may remain in the environment for many years.

Plankton   Microscopic plants and the larvae of tiny animals that live in the surface layers of a body of water.

Predator   An animal that preys on other animals.

Shaman   A kind of priest or healer who is recognized to have contact with the spirit world.

Snowmobile   A motorized scooter that can pull a sled.

Taboo   Something that is banned for social or religious reasons.

Translucent   Something is translucent if it lets light through without your being able to see through it.

Tundra   A flat, treeless Arctic region where only small plants, mosses, and shrubs can grow.

Umiak   An open skin-covered boat.

Glossary of Inuit Words

Angakkuq   A shaman; a type of priest or healer who claims to have contact with the spirit world.

Igloolik   The name of an Inuit community in Canada's eastern Arctic.

Illu   A house of any kind.

Illuviga   Dome-shaped shelter built from bricks of snow.

Inuit   The name the Inuit people use for themselves. It means people or human beings.

Inuk A person. The singular of Inuit.
Inuktitut The language spoken by the Inuit of northern Alaska, Canada, and Greenland.
Nuna Land, a country, or the planet Earth.
Nunavut Our Land. The name given by the Inuit to both a territory and a land claim in the Canadian Arctic.

Qallunaaq The Inuit name for white people.
Upernaallit Those who arrive in spring. The name given to the nineteenth-century whalers by the Inuit.
Yupik The language spoken by the Inuit of southwest Alaska.

Further Reading

Ekoomiak, Normee. *Arctic Memories*. H. Holt, 1990

Damas, David. *Handbook of North American Indians*, *Vol. 5*, *The Arctic*. Smithsonian Institution Press, 1984

George, Jean C. *Julie of the Wolves*. Harper Collins, 1972

Hahn, Elizabeth. *Inuit*. Rourke, 1990

Hughes, Jill. *Arctic Lands*. Watts, 1987

James, Barbara. *Conserving the Polar Regions*. Steck-Vaughn, 1991

Paulsen, Gary. Dogsong. Macmillan, 1985

Vickery, Eugene L. *The Ramiluk Stories: Adventures of an Eskimo Family in the Prehistoric Arctic*. Stonehaven, 1989

Further Information

Department of Renewable Resources
Field Service Division
P.O. Box 1320
Yellowknife, NWT
Canada X1A 2L9

Tungavik Federation of Nunavut
Suite 800
130 Slater Street
Ottawa, Ontario
Canada K1P 6E2

Indigenous Survival International
47 Clarence Street
Suite 300
Ottawa, Ontario
Canada K1N 9K1

Tusarliivik
Greenland Home Rule, Information Service
P.O. Box 1020
DK 3900 Nuuk
Greenland

Inuit Circumpolar Conference
Silarsuarmi Inuit Katuttiqatigiifingat
Post Boks 204
Godthaab 3900, Greenland

Index

*Numbers in **bold** refer to pictures in addition to text.*